Welcome
TO
4 Panel Botanical Designs
- A Home Decor Coloring Book -

92 Botanical Designs divided into 4 panels on 23 pages

The designs in this book are adaptations of original botanical art of Curtis Botanicals – a magazine publication that began in the late 1700's and ended in the early 1800's.

We have painstakingly digitally removed the water spots, foxing and other page damage from original images in our possession in order to convert these images to black and white drawings for you to color.

Some designs in this book are relatively easy to complete while you may find other designs a bit more intricate and challenging.

There is no right or wrong color or design so be as creative or traditional as you'd like. Mix and match colors to coordinate with the decor in the different rooms of your home.

When completed and ready for framing, these 8 x 10 pages will fit perfectly into the standard opening of an 11 x 14 mat.

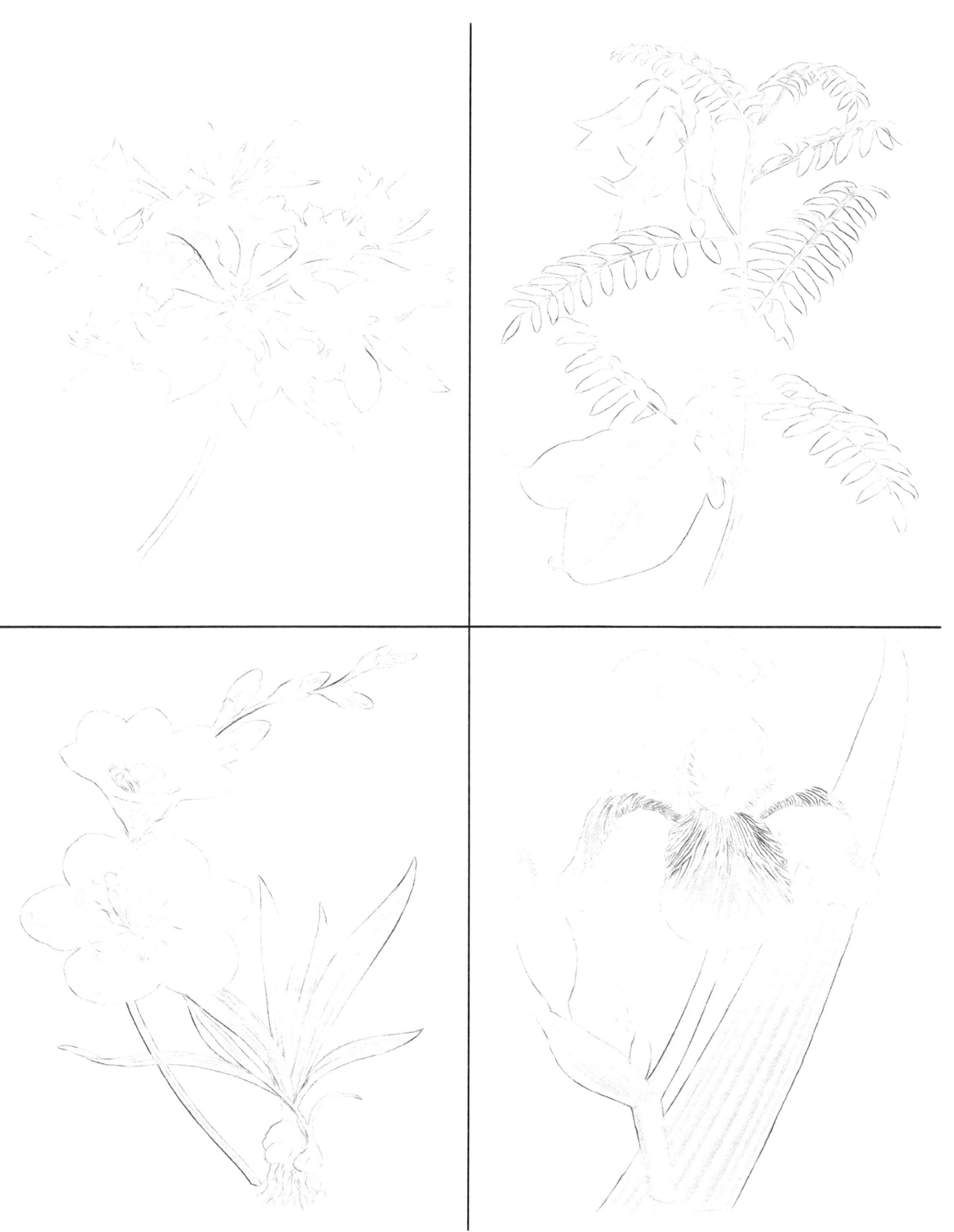

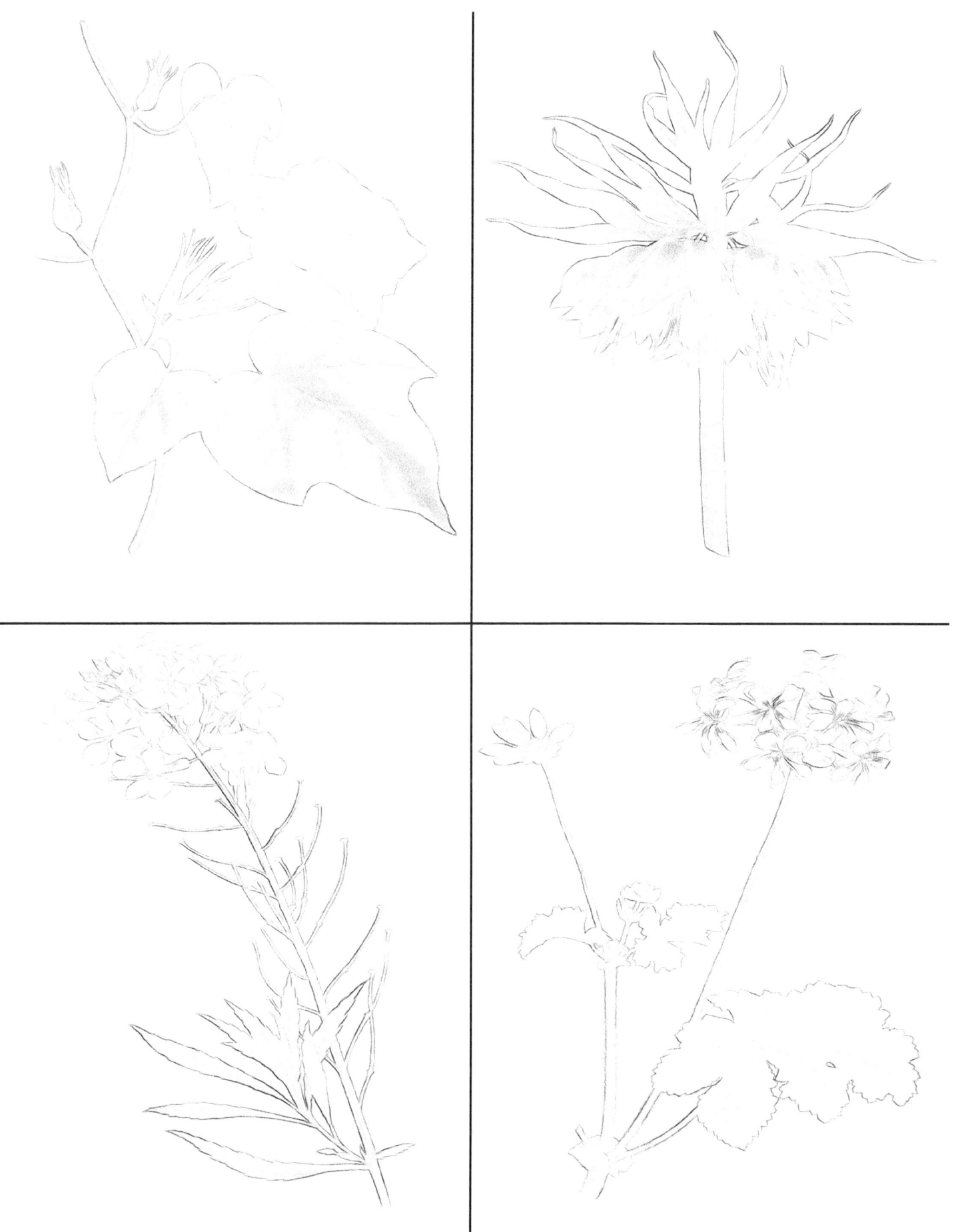

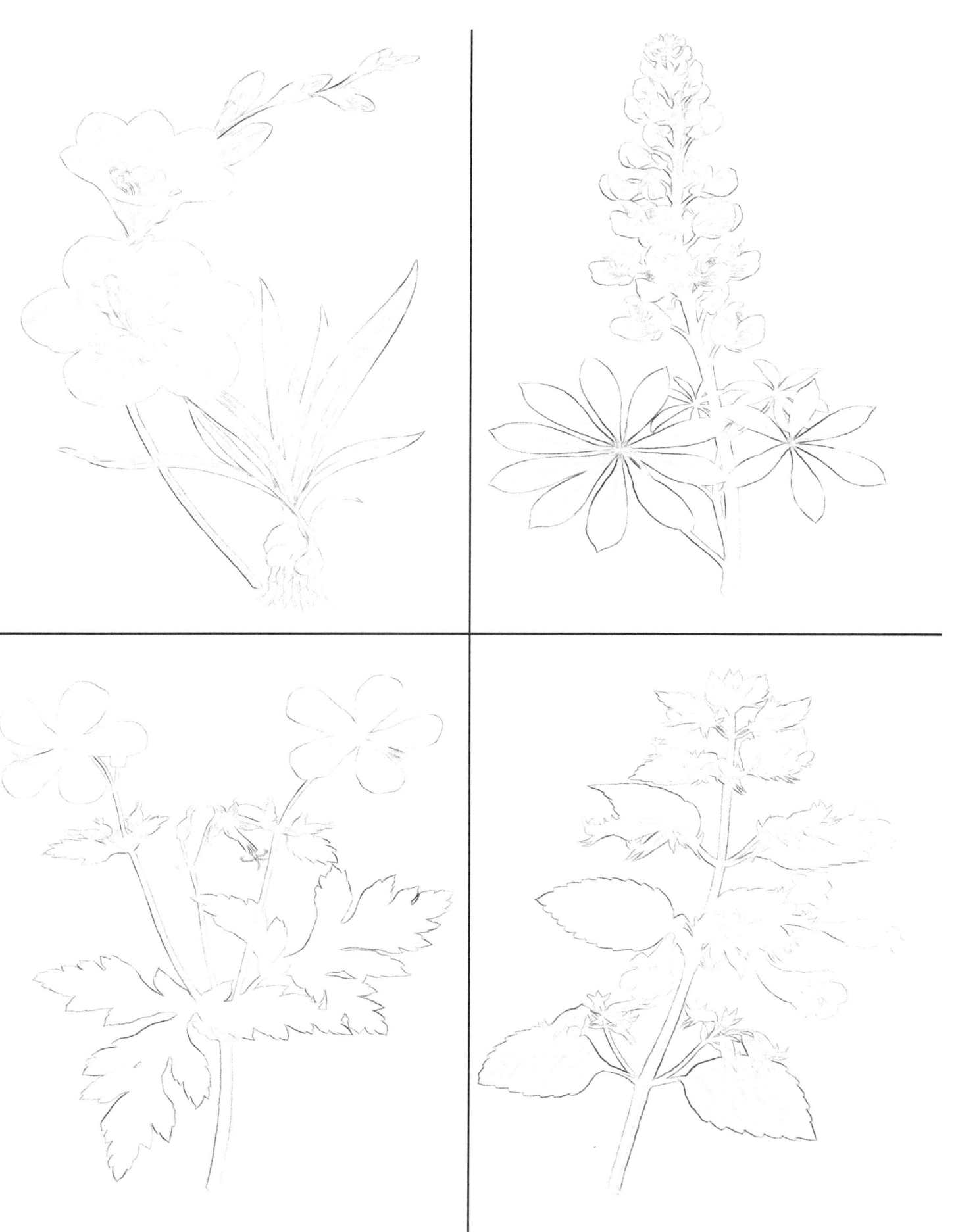

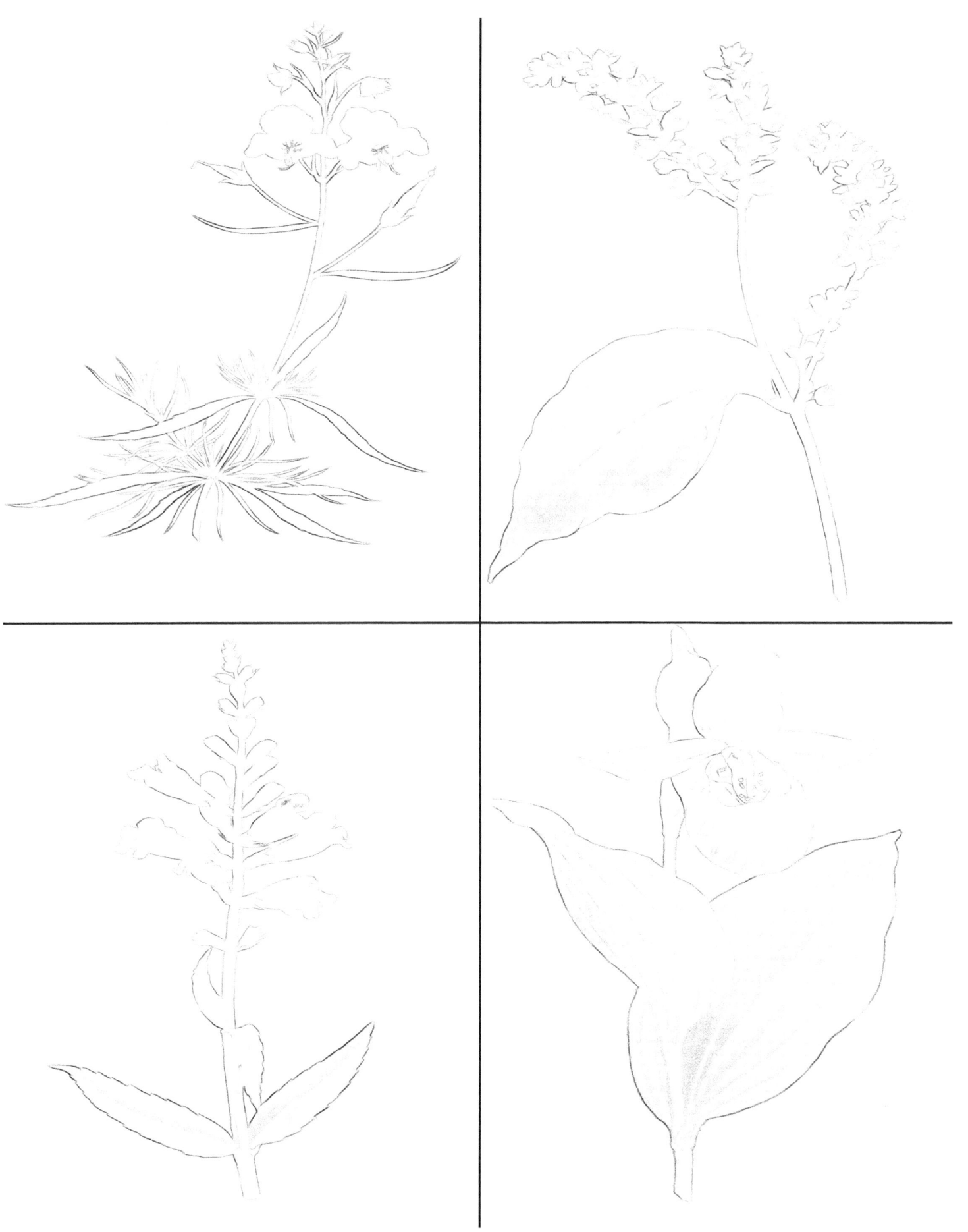

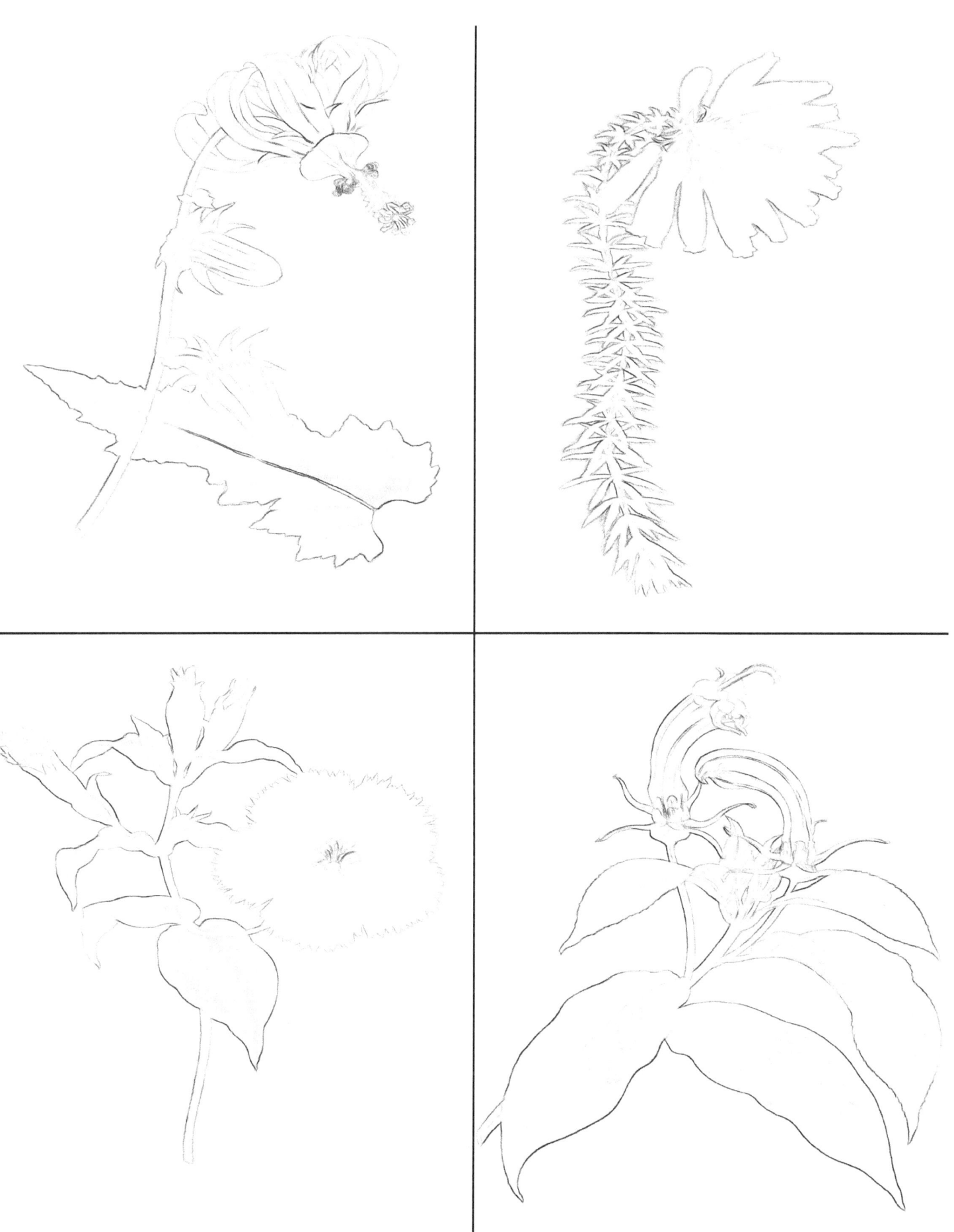

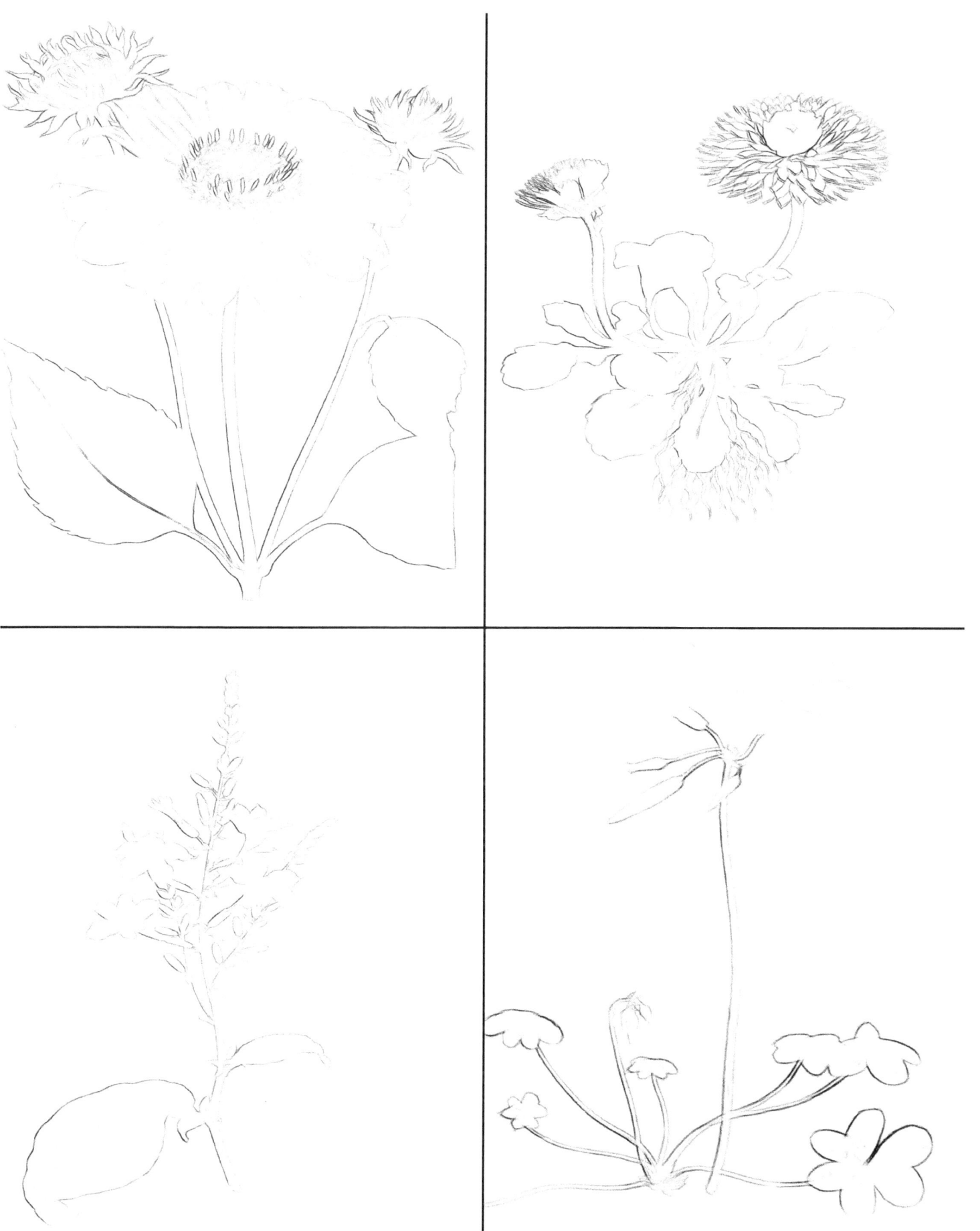

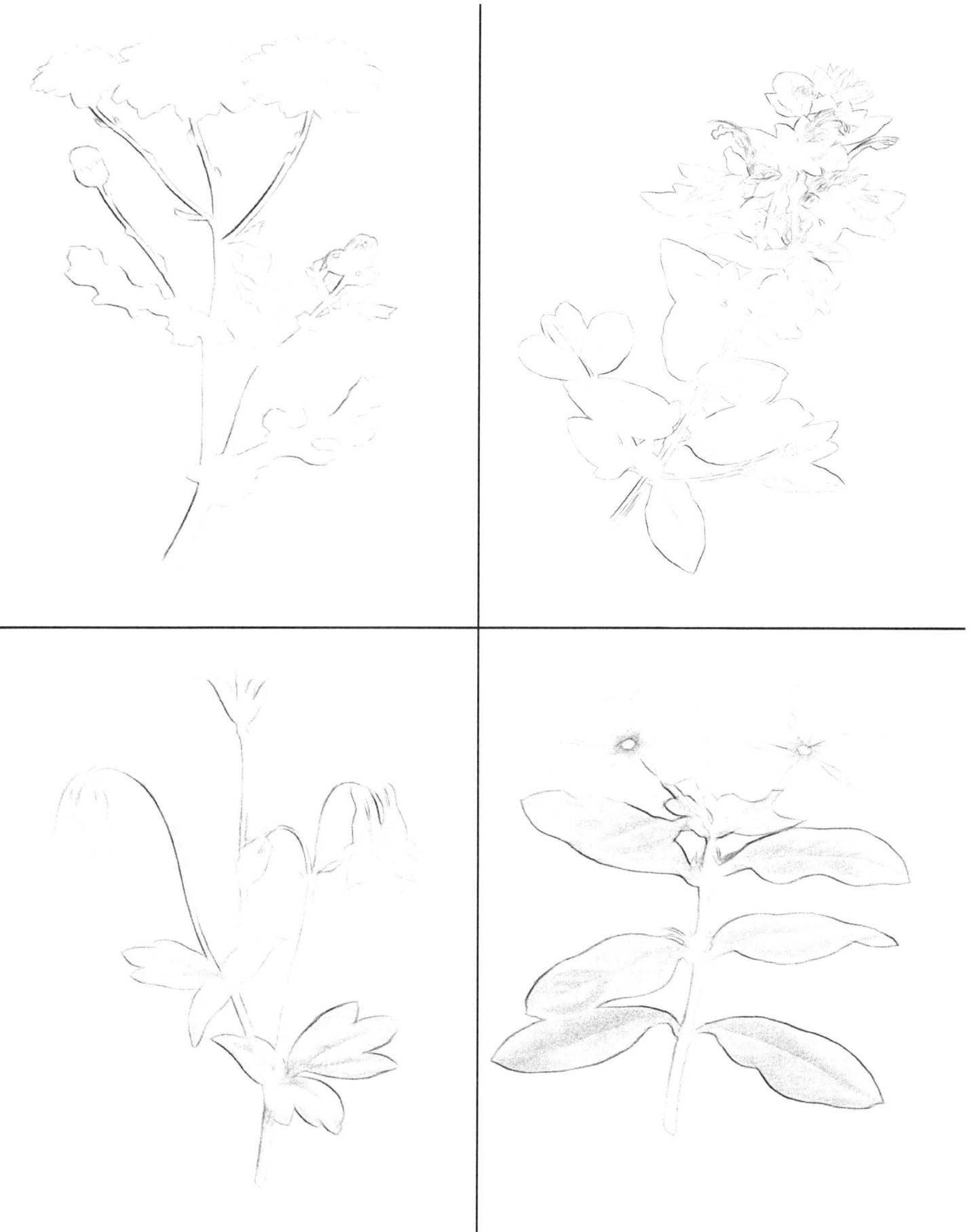

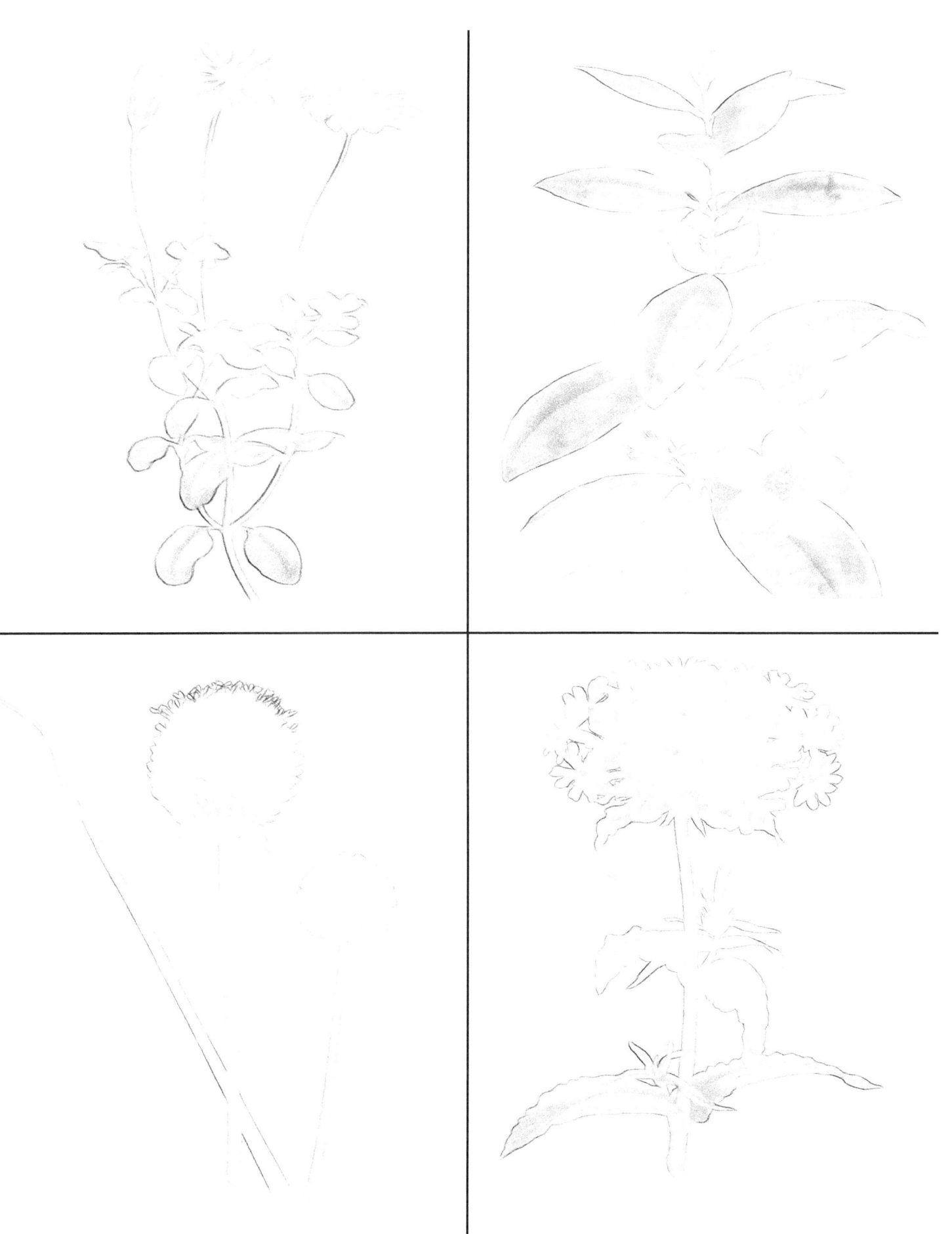

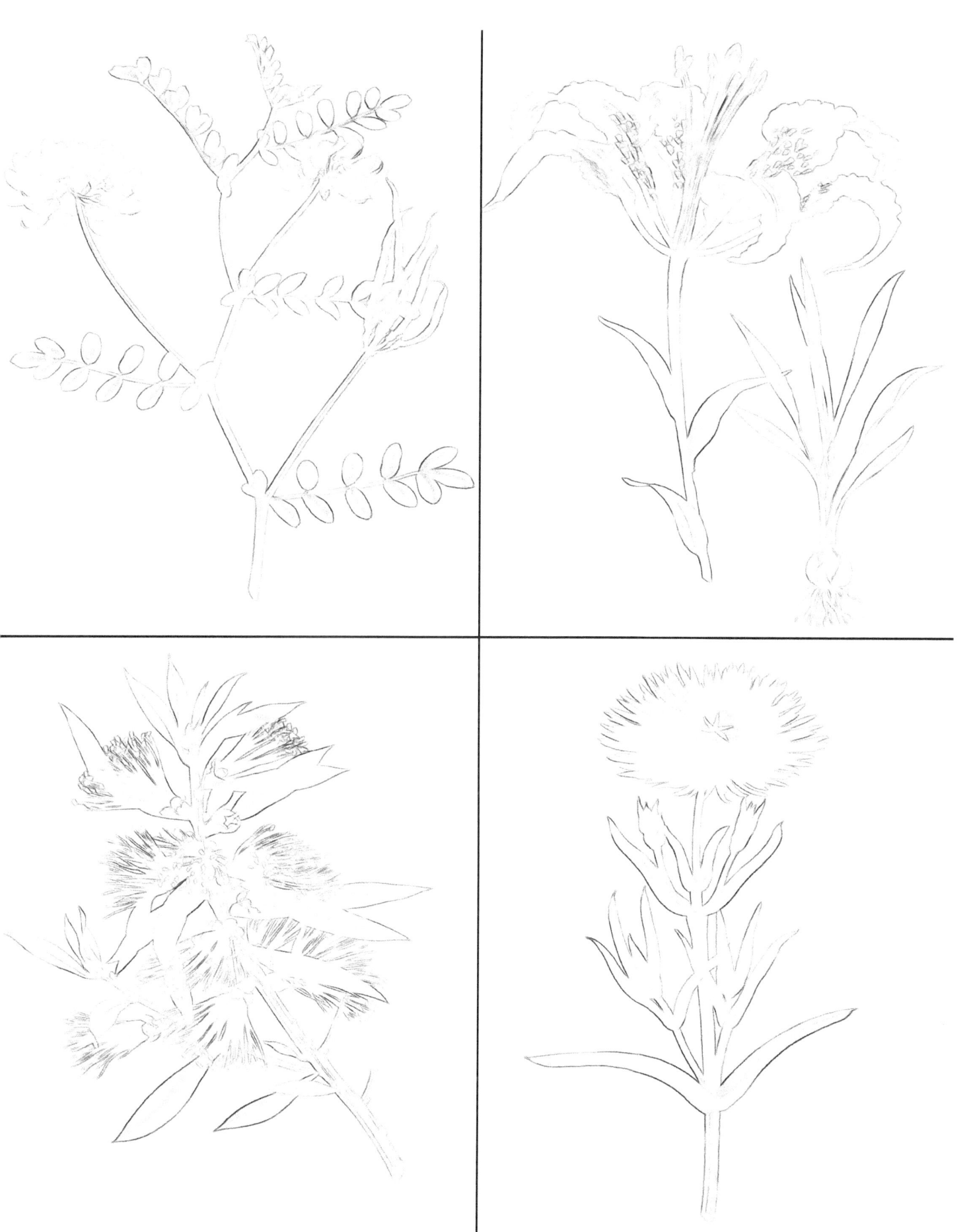

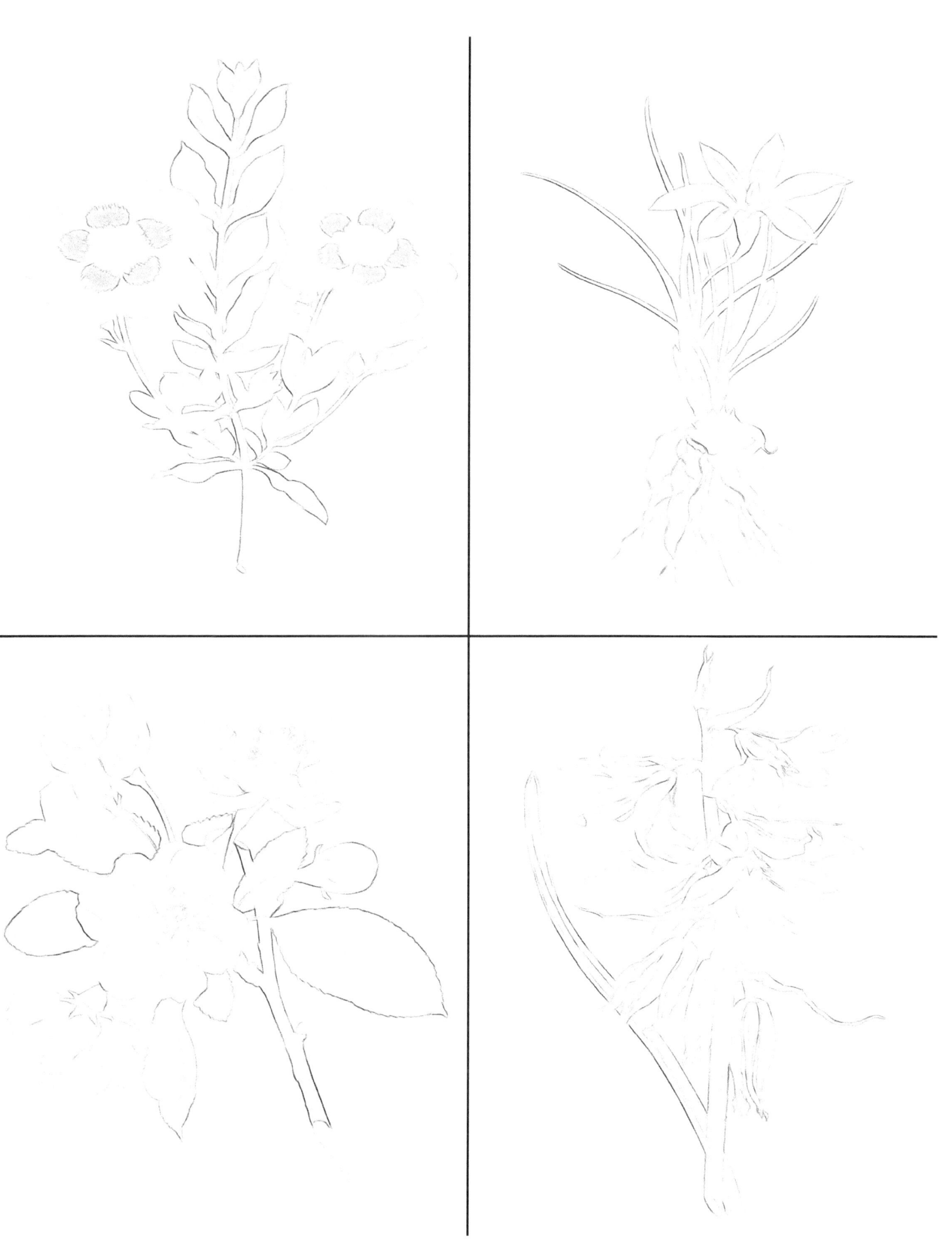

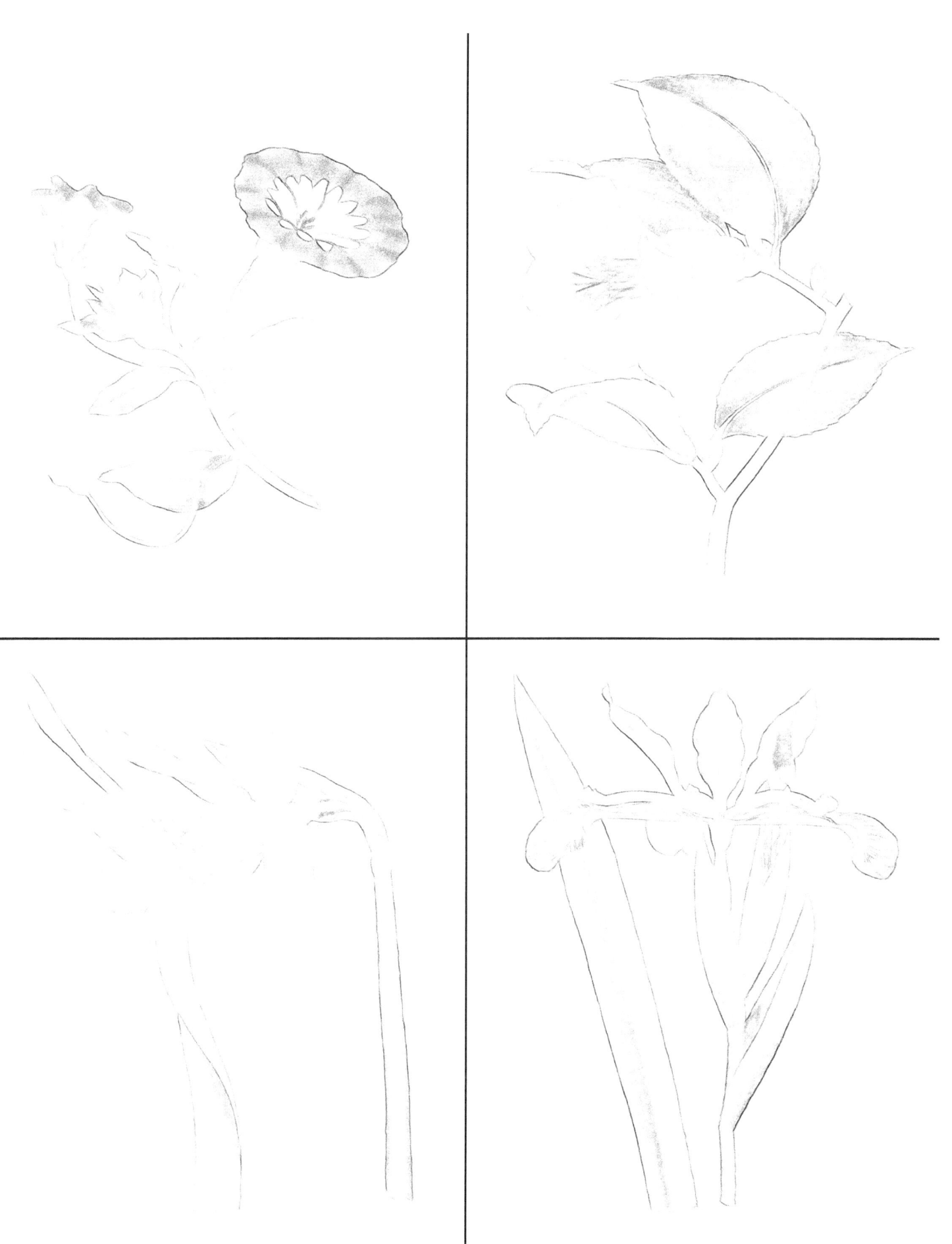

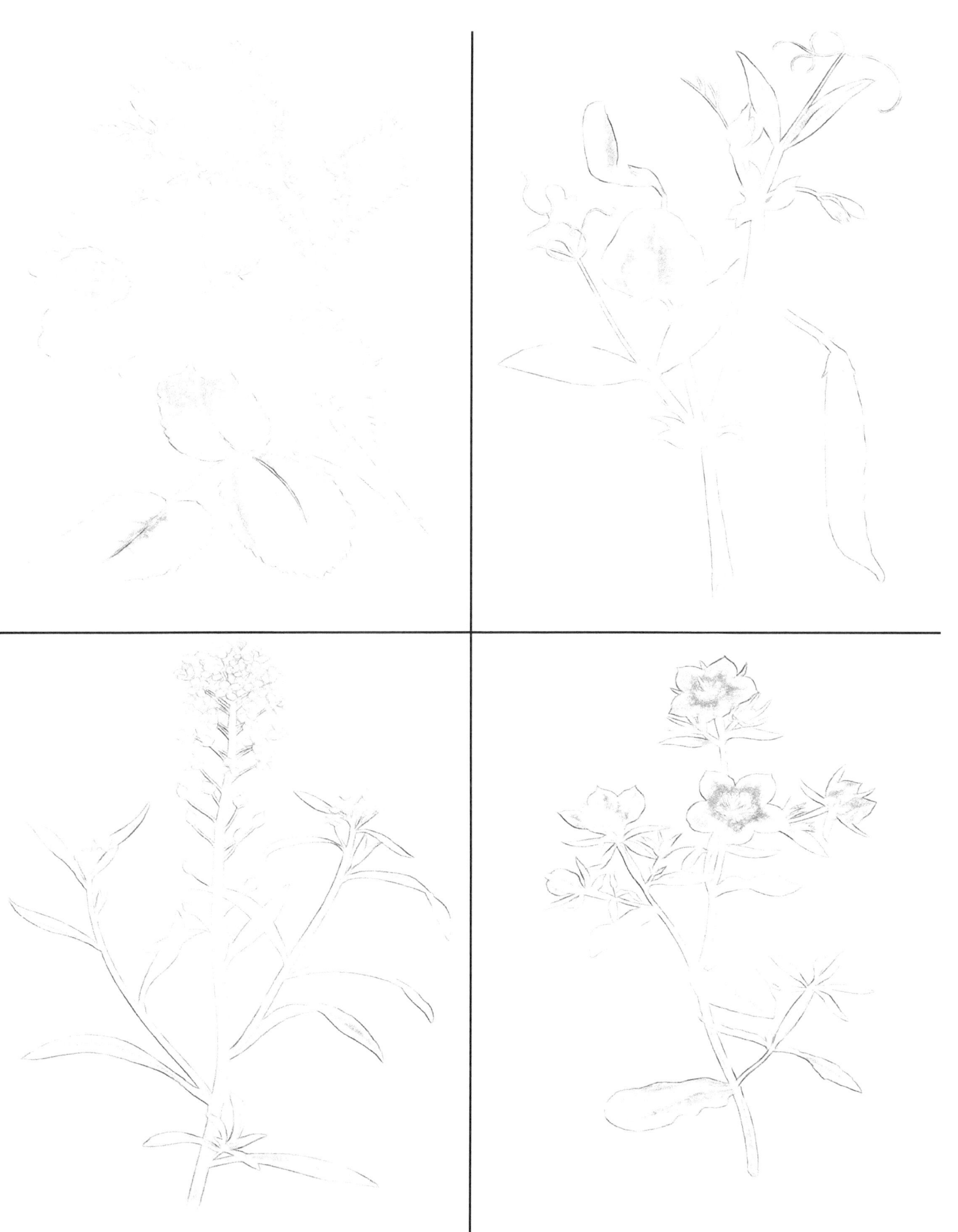

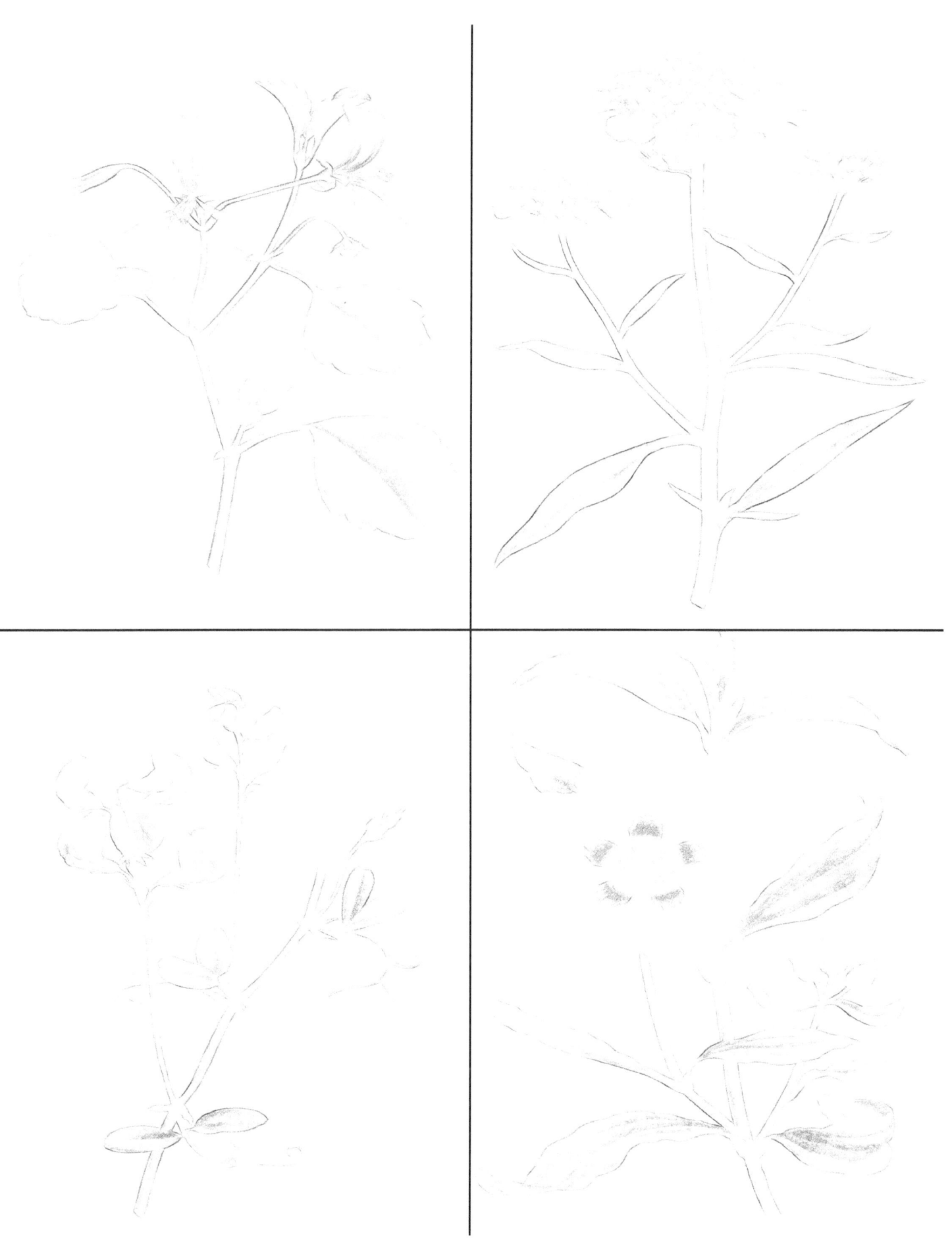

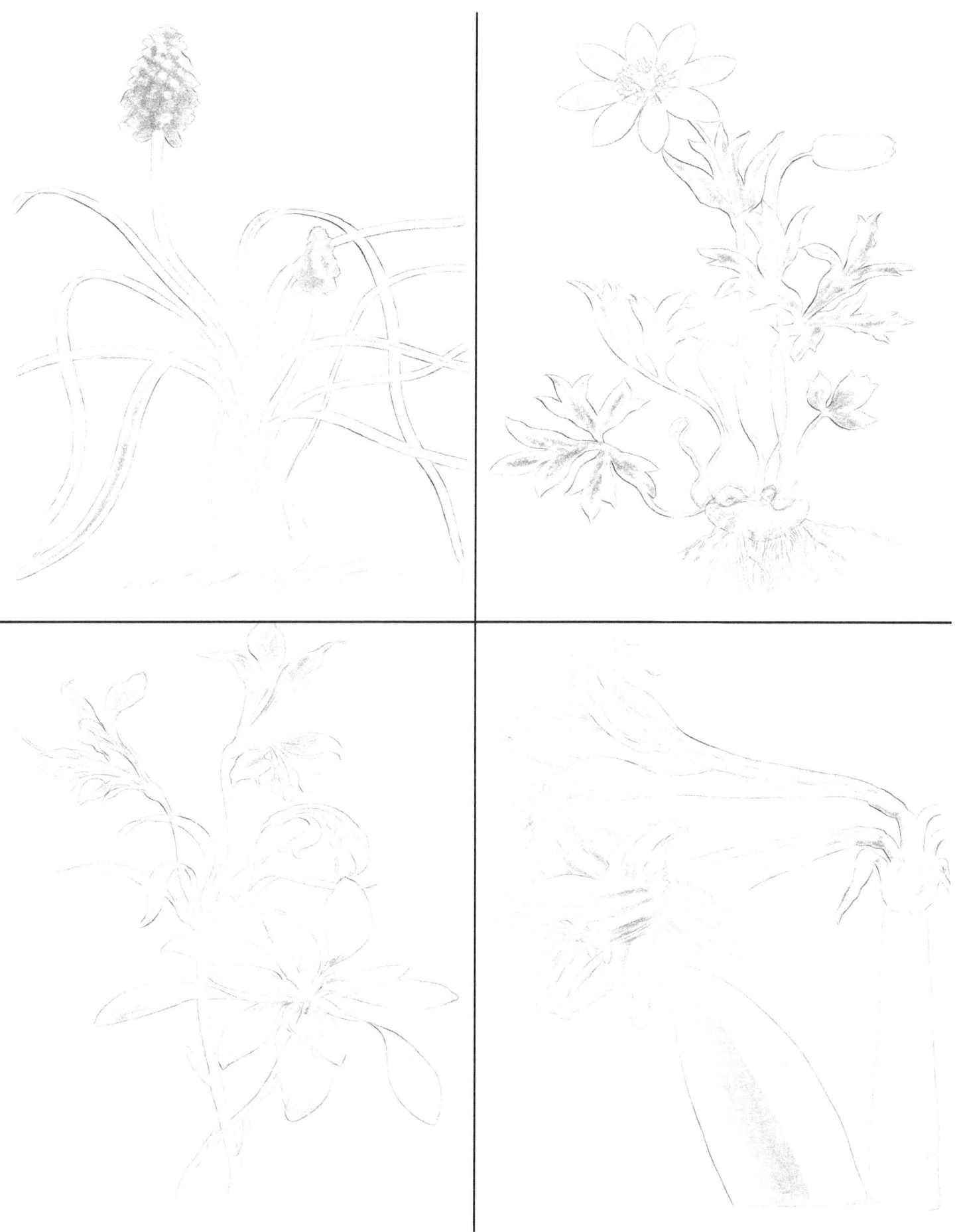

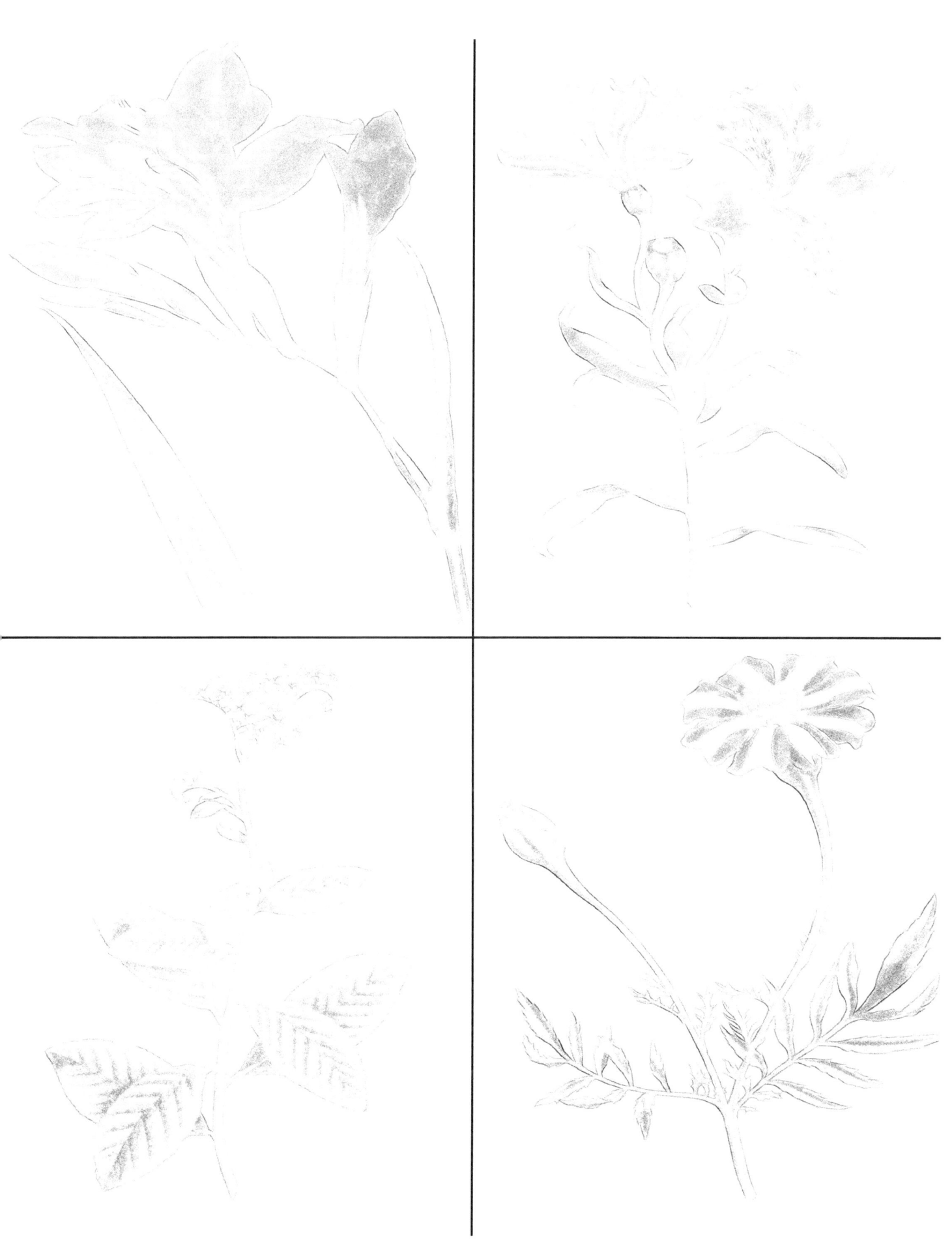

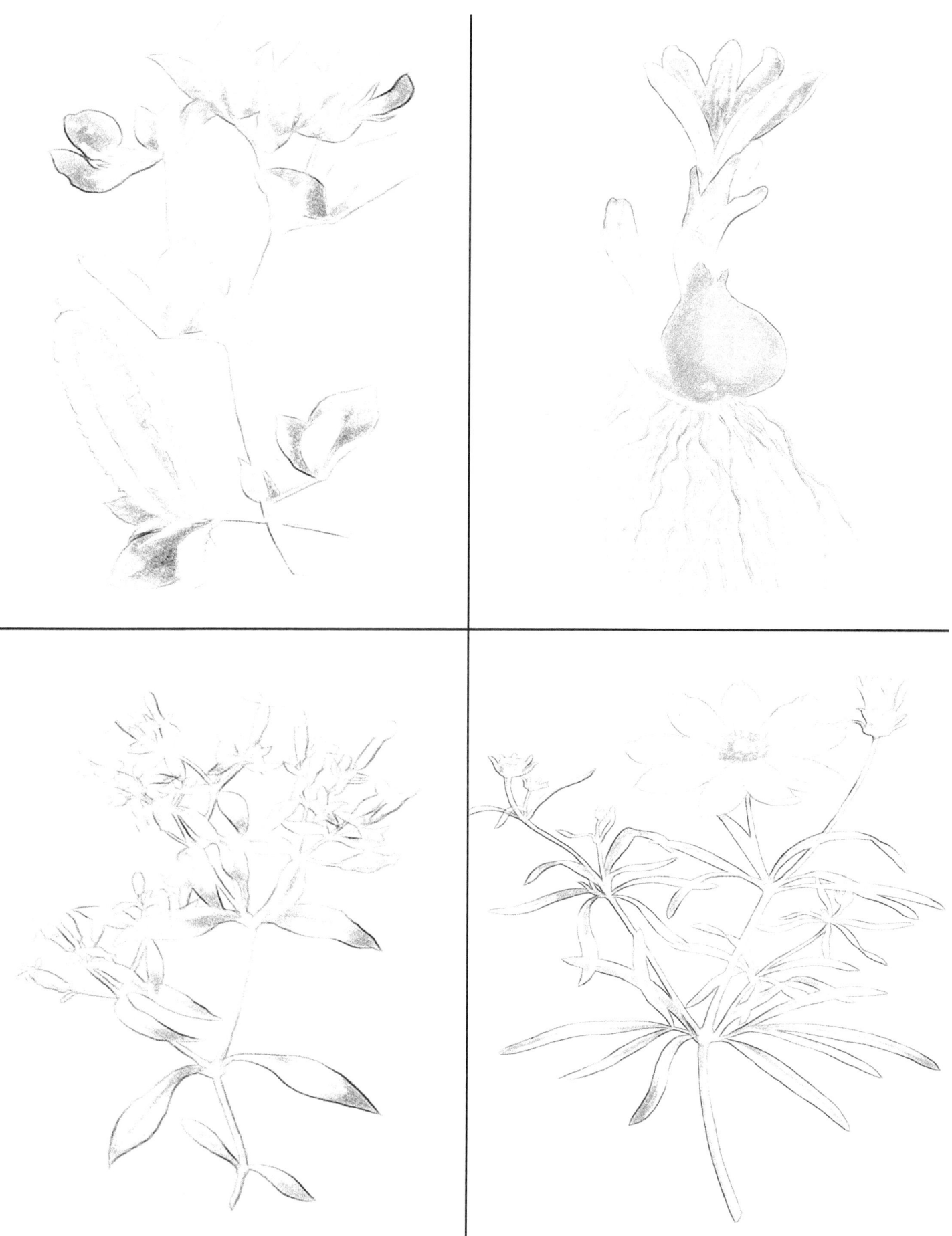

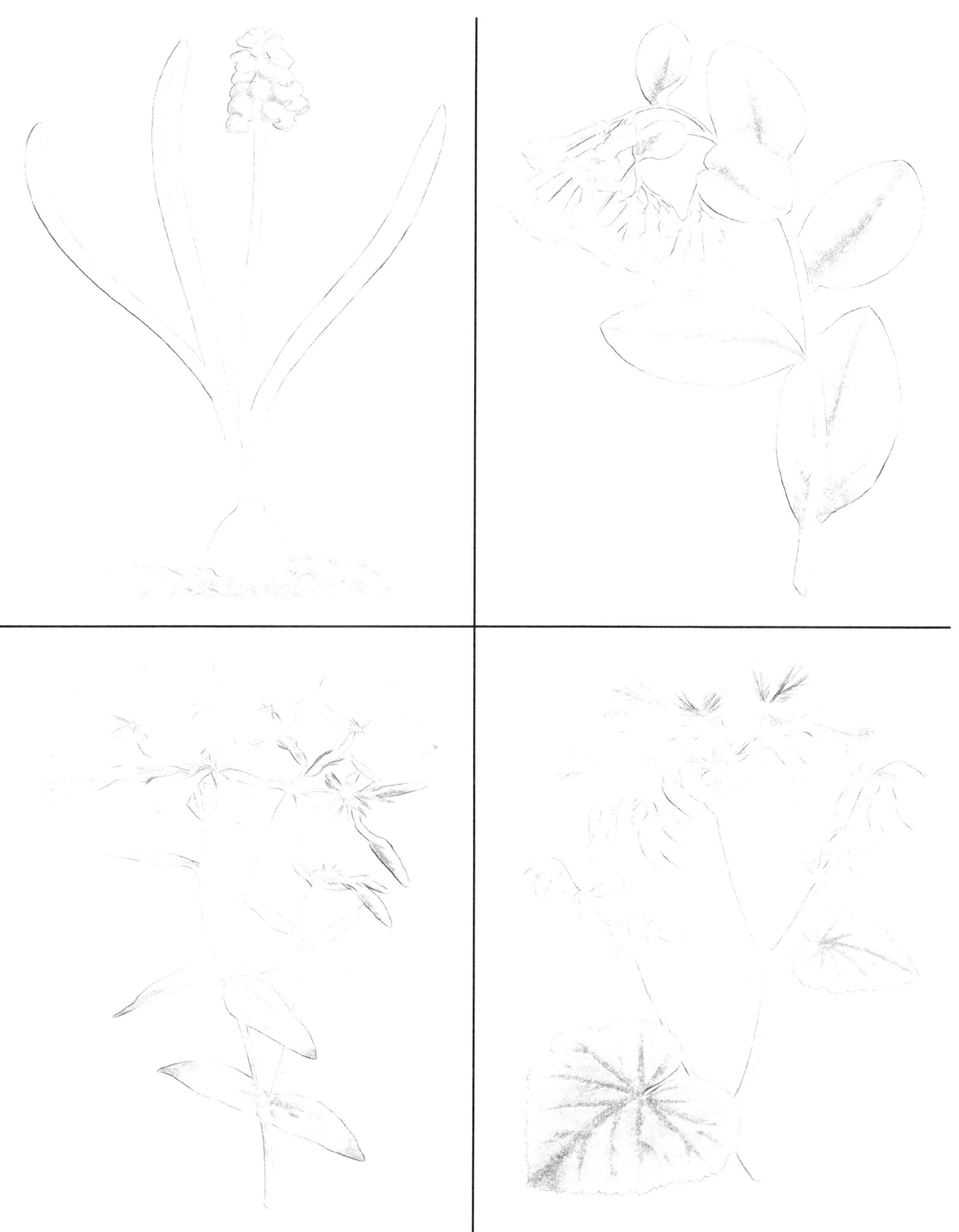

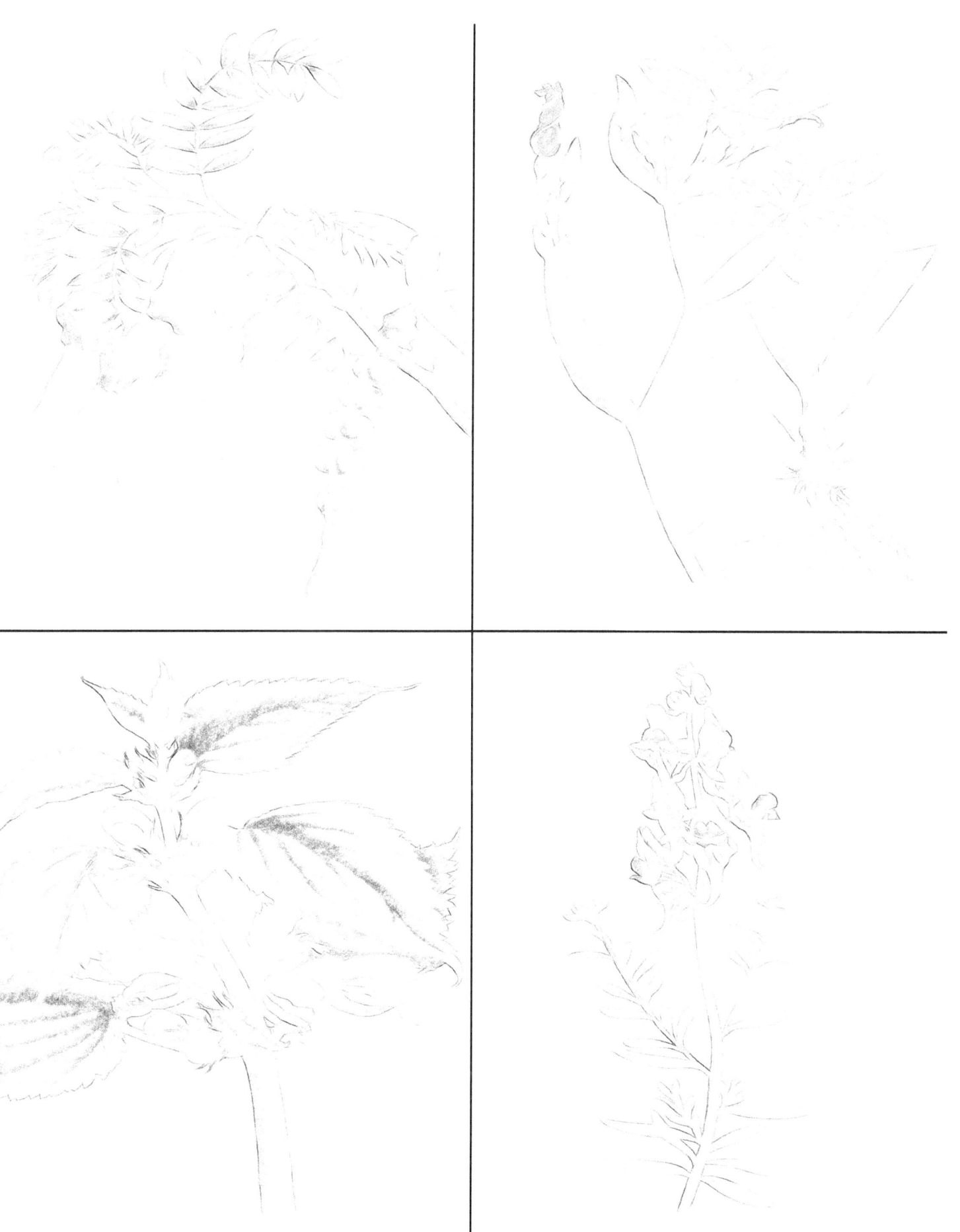

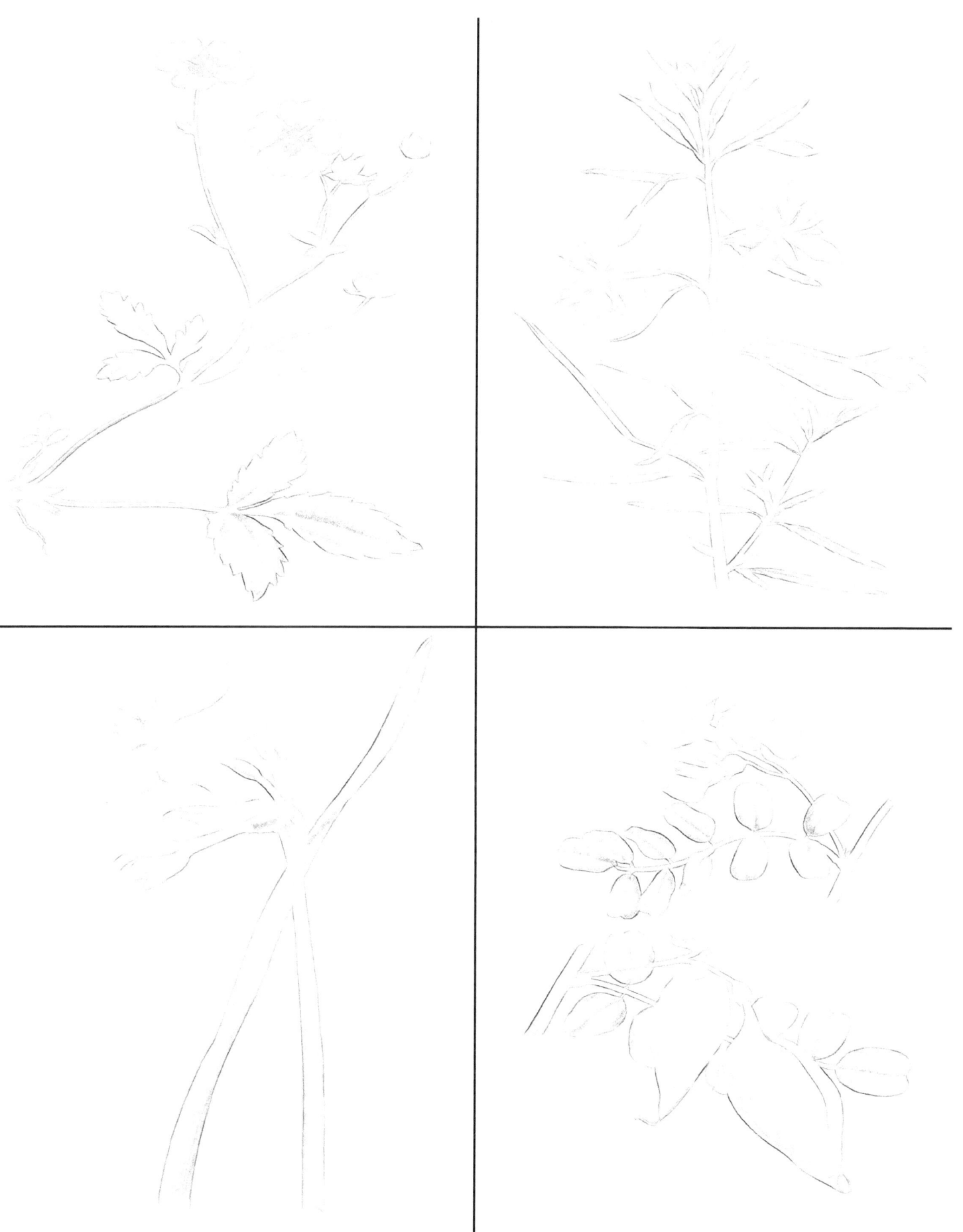

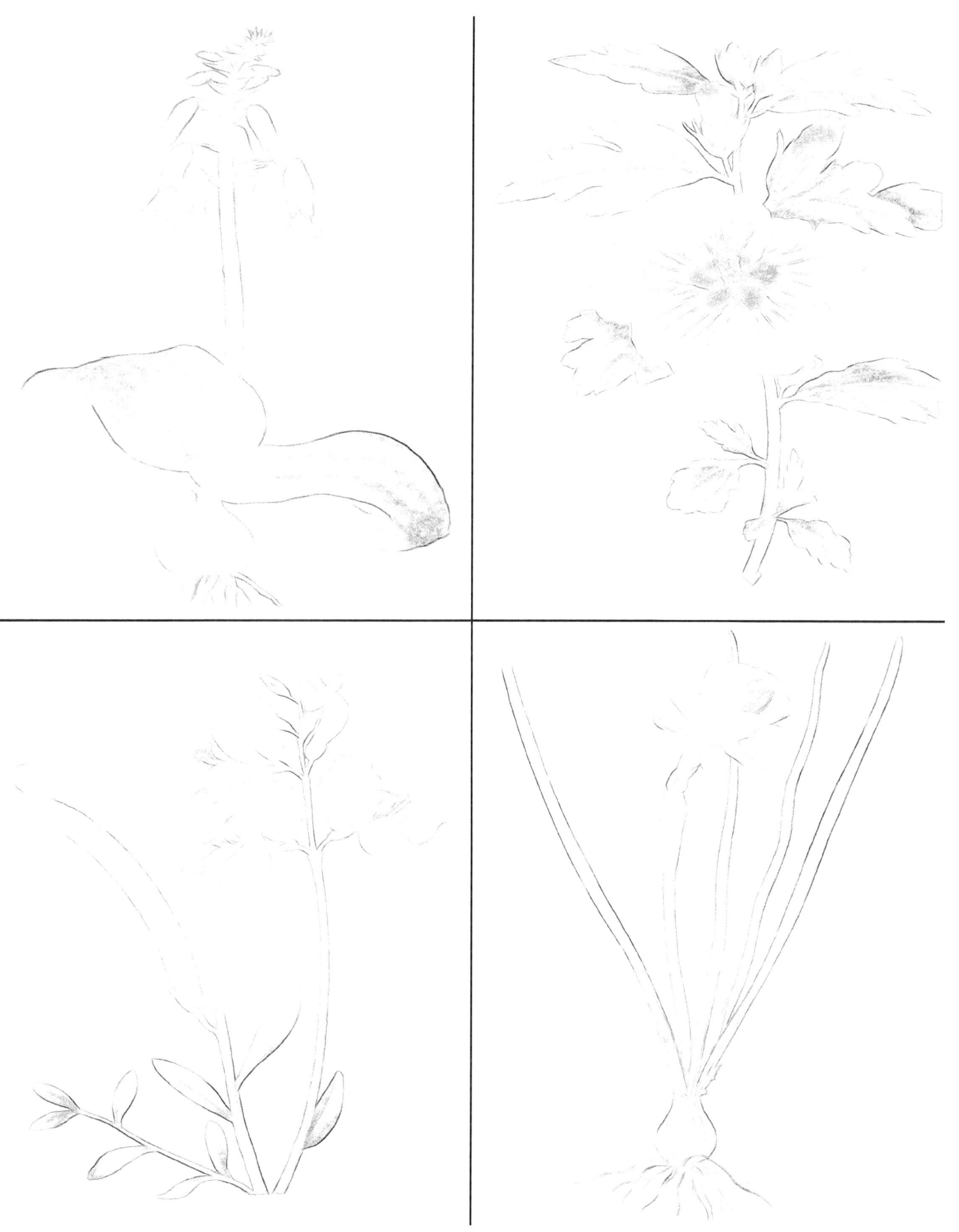

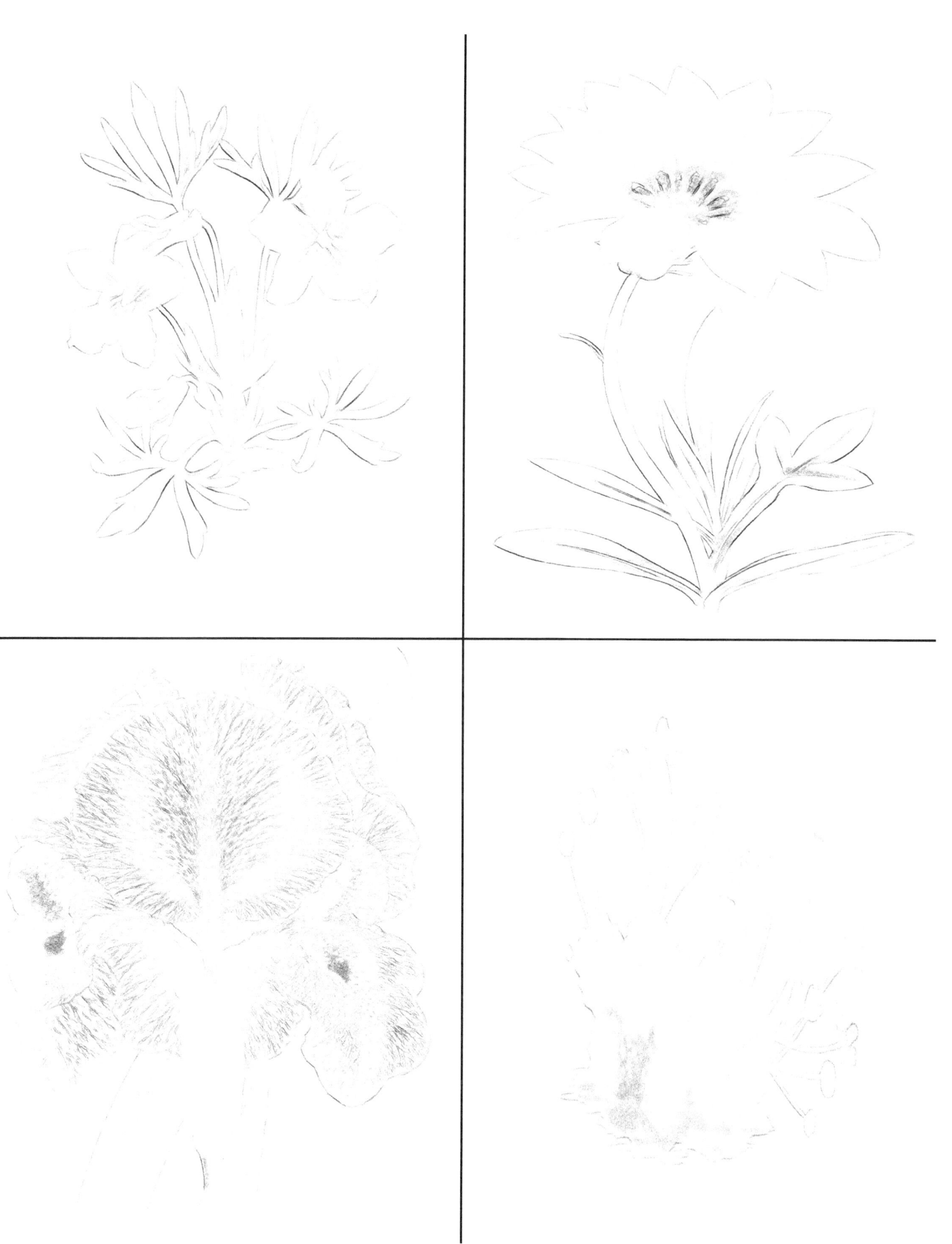

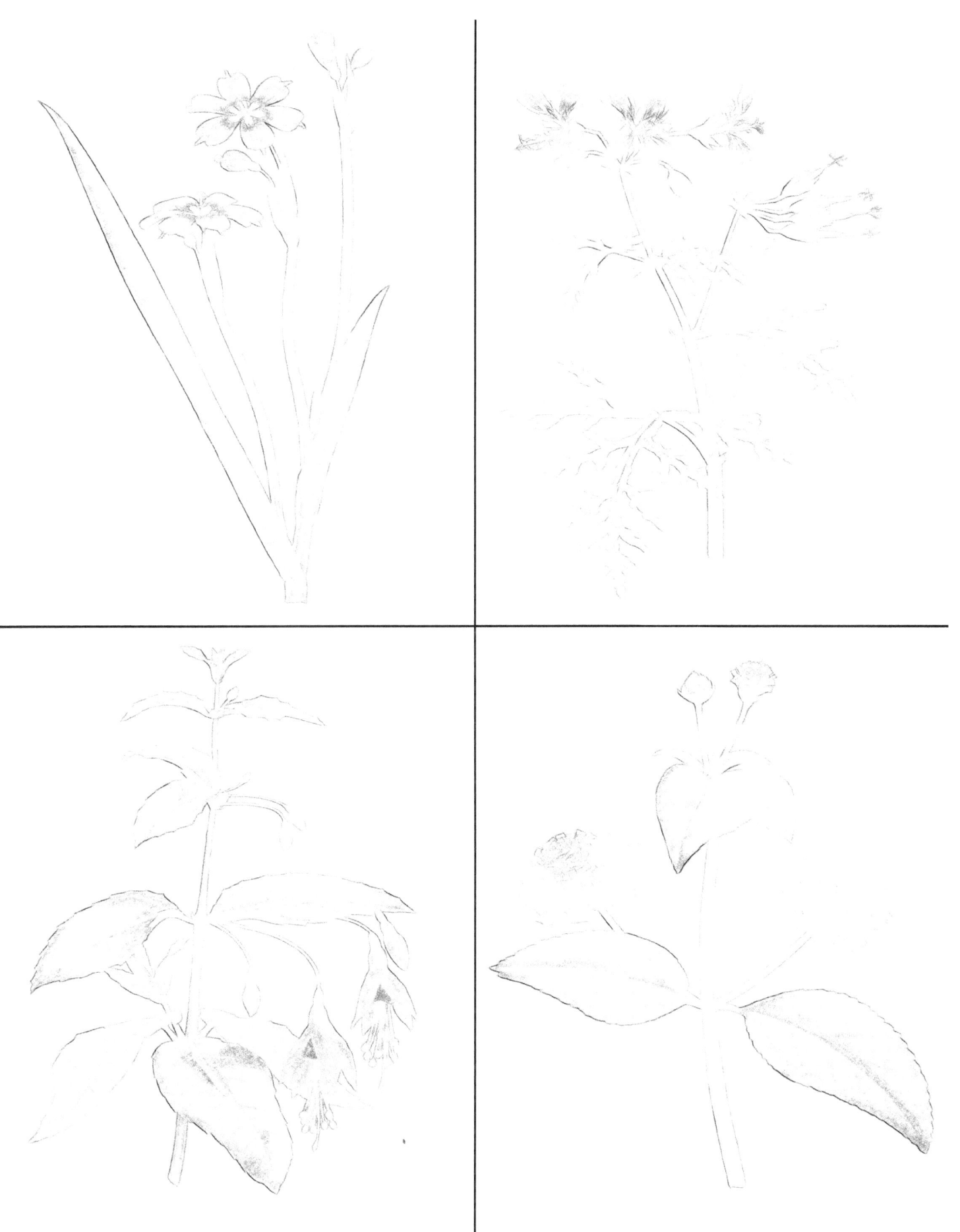

www.ingramcontent.com/pod-product-compliance
Lightning Source LLC
Chambersburg PA
CBHW080615180526
45168CB00007B/2924